Oxford First Encyclopedia

Earth
and the
Universe

Andrew Langley

OXFORD

OXFORD
UNIVERSITY PRESS

Great Clarendon Street, Oxford OX2 6DP

Oxford University Press is a department of the University of Oxford.
It furthers the University's objective of excellence in research, scholarship,
and education by publishing worldwide in

Oxford New York

Auckland Bangkok Buenos Aires Cape Town Chennai
Dar es Salaam Delhi Hong Kong Istanbul Karachi Kolkata
Kuala Lumpur Madrid Melbourne Mexico City Mumbai Nairobi
São Paulo Shanghai Singapore Taipei Tokyo Toronto

with an associated company in Berlin

Oxford is a registered trade mark of Oxford University Press
in the UK and in certain other countries

© Andrew Langley 1999, 2002

The moral rights of the author have been asserted

Database right Oxford University Press (maker)

First published in 1999
Second edition 2002

British Library Cataloguing in Publication Data available

ISBN 0-19-910973-7

10 9 8 7 6 5 4 3

Printed in Malaysia

Contents

The Earth

The Earth is a huge ball that spins round and round in space. Its surface is covered by water and land. If you could look down at the Earth from up in space, you would see lots of clouds swirling over its surface. Through the clouds you would see the blue colour of the oceans and seas. Nearly two-thirds of the Earth is covered with water. A layer of air, called the atmosphere, surrounds the Earth.

Sun's rays

North Pole

daytime

Equator

axis

South Pole

Day and night

The Earth takes 24 hours to turn all the way round – that is one day and one night. When your country is facing the Sun, it is daytime for you. But as the Earth turns you away from the Sun, everything around you grows darker. During the darkness of the night, your country faces away from the Sun. When you wake up and everything is light again, this is a new day.

△ The Earth always spins around an imaginary line through its middle that we call the Earth's axis. The axis runs through the North and South Poles. Right around the middle of the Earth on the outside is another imaginary line, called the Equator.

Our world

From space, the Earth's surface looks smooth – but it isn't really. It has hills and valleys and mountains and gorges, even under the sea. This map is flat, but it shows the most important features on the Earth's surface.

▷ All the land in the world is divided up into seven big areas called "continents". They are Africa, Asia, Antarctica, Europe, North America, Oceania and South America. The continents are shown in different colours on the map.

Arctic Ocean

ROCKY MOUNTAINS

North America

North Atlantic Ocean

Pacific Ocean

Tropic of Cancer

Equator

Tropic of Capricorn

Angel Falls

Amazon River

ANDES

South America

Atacama Desert

Guallatiri

0   1050   2100   3150   4200 km

Antarctica

South Pole

Antarctica

Antarctic Circle

◁ One continent, Antarctica, has to be a strange shape to fit on the big world map. This map shows its proper shape.

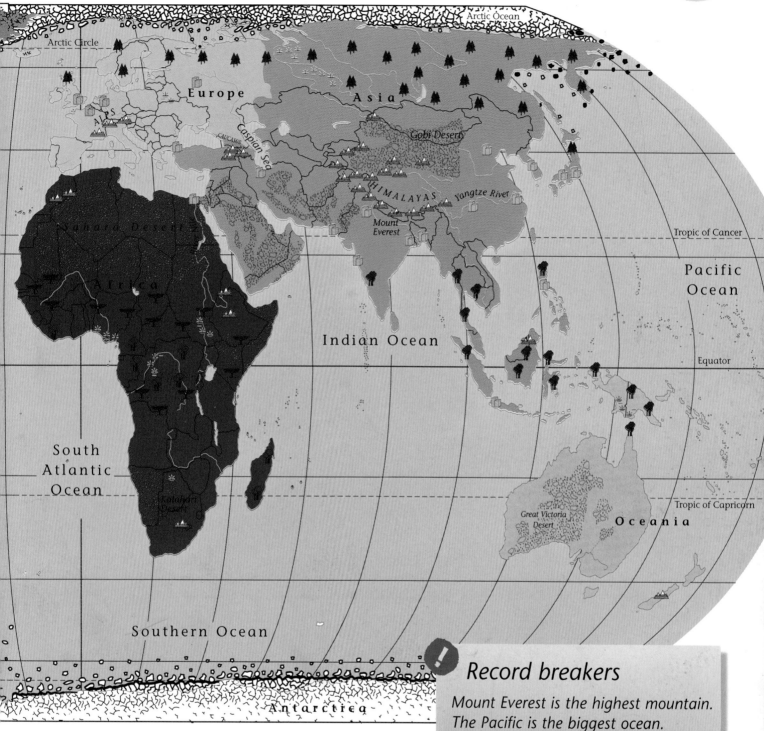

Arctic Ocean

Arctic Circle

Europe

Asia

ALPS

CAUCASUS

Caspian Sea

Gobi Desert

Sahara Desert

HIMALAYAS

Yangtze River

Mount Everest

Tropic of Cancer

Africa

Pacific Ocean

Indian Ocean

Equator

South Atlantic Ocean

Kalahari Desert

Great Victoria Desert

Oceania

Tropic of Capricorn

Southern Ocean

Antarctica

Record breakers

Mount Everest is the highest mountain.
The Pacific is the biggest ocean.
The Nile is the longest river.
The Caspian Sea is the biggest lake.
Angel Falls is the highest waterfall.
Guallatiri is the highest volcano.
Greenland is the largest island.
The Sahara is the biggest desert.

Key

desert		high mountains	
marsh		cold forest	
ice on land		savannah	
ice on the sea		hot forest	
country boundary		very large cities	

Sky above, Earth below

We live on the outside part of the Earth. Around and above us is the air we breathe. Beneath us is the Earth's crust, or outer layer. The crust is made of hard rocks, which have been wrinkled and bent to make mountains and valleys.

The crust is the Earth's outer layer. It is much thinner than the other layers.

Under the crust lies the mantle. The rocks in the mantle are red-hot, and some of them are so soft that they ooze about.

The rocks in the outer core are so hot that they have melted into a liquid.

The inner core lies at the centre of the Earth. The weight of all the rocks above the inner core squashes it into a solid ball.

To the centre of the Earth

Can you dig right down to the centre of the Earth? If you tried, you would soon find it getting much too hot. As you go deeper, the rocks become hotter – and hotter! Scientists think that the very middle of the Earth is 60 times hotter than boiling water.

A blanket of air

The Earth is wrapped up in an invisible layer of air called the atmosphere. Without this air, there would be no living things on Earth. The atmosphere acts like a blanket. It keeps us warm by trapping the heat of the Sun. And the air in the atmosphere contains important gases such as oxygen, which we breathe to keep us alive. The atmosphere also acts like sunglasses. It stops some of the Sun's harmful rays from reaching the ground.

satellite

Space Shuttle

gas balloon

hot-air balloon

aeroplane

△ We cannot explore deep inside the Earth, but we can travel up into the atmosphere, in balloons and aircraft.

◁ The atmosphere has several different layers. Higher up, the air gets thinner and colder, and there is less oxygen to breathe. In the very highest layers there is hardly any air at all.

The moving Earth

Imagine what it would be like if the ground beneath your feet suddenly started to move! This is what happens during an earthquake. The top layer of the Earth bends and shakes. When a volcano erupts, it can be even more dramatic. Melted rock from under the surface bursts out through a crack in the Earth's crust in a red hot stream.

Volcanoes

Deep under the Earth's surface are pockets of hot, melted rock. If there is a crack in the surface, this hot rock forces its way up and out of the crack. Tonnes of fiery, melted rock called "lava" blast out of the crack. As the lava flows away from the crack, it cools down and hardens into new rock. This new rock piles up around the crack to form a volcano.

▽ An erupting volcano is a terrifying sight. Lava bursts out from the top, and enormous clouds of ash and steam choke the air. Sometimes, a volcano can even explode and be completely blown apart.

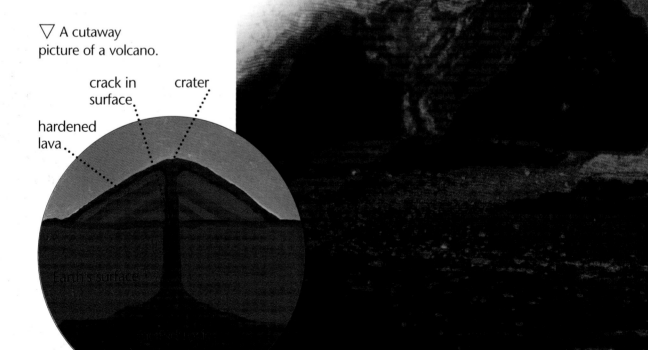

▽ A cutaway picture of a volcano.

crack in surface

crater

hardened lava

Earth's surface

The Earth

Earthquakes

When the Earth starts to shake violently, huge cracks open up in the Earth's surface. Buildings fall down and roads split apart. Bridges break in two and trees are ripped out of the ground. The land tilts and sends loose rock sliding downhill. Earthquakes under the sea can cause enormous waves that race to the shore and flood the land. These giant waves are called tsunamis.

The biggest bang

Over 100 years ago, in 1883, a volcanic island in Indonesia blew up. It was called Krakatau. The explosion of Krakatau made one of the loudest bangs ever. People heard it over 4800 kilometres away! A huge cloud of ash blotted out the sun for two whole days.

△ A volcano may not erupt for many years, or it may stop erupting altogether. Thousands of years ago, this lake was part of a huge volcano. But the volcano stopped erupting, and now the crater where lava once poured out has filled with water.

11

Shaping the landscape

We think of a mountain as something big and solid, and it always looks exactly the same. Yet a mountain is changing every day. Wind, cold and water are wearing it away, cutting and carving the rock into new shapes. All around us, the landscape is slowly changing. The land is always being worn away somewhere. At the same time, new land is being made somewhere else.

Wearing away rocks

The weather can break down rocks in different ways. Water pours into cracks in the rock and freezes. The ice splits off small pieces of rock. Rivers cut away the land to make valleys and gorges. In hot dry places, the wind blows sand that scrapes away at rocks – just like sandpaper. And the sea's waves pull up pebbles and throw them at the cliffs, wearing away more rocks.

rain and ice wear away mountains

river carries away pieces of rock

cliffs are worn away by the sea

▷ This desert landscape in the USA is made up of soft rocks and hard rocks. Over millions of years, the soft rocks have been worn away more quickly than the hard rocks, leaving the hard rocks sticking up in strange shapes.

Making new land

Although rocks are broken up, they do not vanish. Instead they are moved somewhere else. Rivers carry the rocks away, breaking them up into tiny pieces. The rivers flow into lakes and seas. Here, the rock pieces sink down to form a new layer of sand or mud. As time goes by, more and more layers build up on top of each other. This is how new land and rocks are formed.

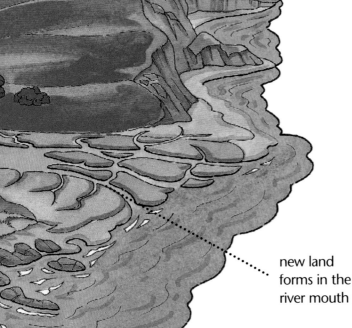

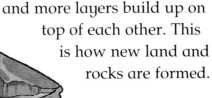
new land forms in the river mouth

Make a mountain

When two different pieces of the Earth's crust push into each other, their surfaces crumple and fold up. This is how mountains are made. You can see how this happens by using two big floppy books (try telephone directories). Put them on a table and push their open ends together. The pages will bend and fold. Some will be pushed downwards, and others upwards. It may look messy – but that is what mountains are!

The weather

What's the weather like today? Is the sun shining, or is the sky full of clouds? Perhaps it is raining, or snowing. Weather can be so many different things – hot or cold, wet or dry, windy or still. And all this weather happens in the atmosphere, the layer of air around the Earth.

Making rain

If you fill the bath with hot water, clouds of steam (water vapour) rise up. When the steam touches something cold, like the window or the mirror, it cools down and turns back into a liquid. This is just what happens when water vapour rises up from the Earth.

The story of rain

Here is the story of how water from the sea becomes rain. The Sun warms up the water, which turns into a gas called water vapour. Wind carries the vapour up into the sky. Here the air is cooler, and the vapour turns into tiny water droplets. These join together to make a cloud. Over high ground, the air gets cooler still. Soon, the droplets grow so heavy that they fall to the ground as rain.

WIND

water vapour makes clouds in cooler air

water vapour rises

sea water

Snow

At the very top of a cloud, the air may be very cold. Here, the water vapour freezes into crystals of ice. These delicate crystals stick together to form flakes of snow. When the snowflakes are heavy enough, they fall towards the ground.

droplets get heavier

R A I N

rainwater runs back to the sea in rivers and streams

Thunder and lightning

After very hot weather we may have a thunderstorm. Tall black clouds appear in the sky. They contain a powerful charge of electricity. When the clouds move close together, or near the ground, giant sparks of electricity fly between them. These are flashes of lightning. Thunder is the noise made by the hot air expanding around the sparks.

Why does wind blow?

The layer of air presses down on the Earth. When the Sun shines, it warms up the Earth. The Earth, in turn, warms the air above it. Warm air does not press down so hard. It starts to rise, and cooler air rushes in to take its place underneath. This is what causes wind.

▽ Wind can blow at many different speeds. Here are some ways of describing them, starting with a calm (no wind at all).

calm

light breeze

strong breeze

gale

hurricane

Climates and seasons

Is it usually cold where you live? Or is it hot and sunny? Some places have a lot of warm sun and not much rain. Some have a lot of sunshine and rain. Other places are cold all year round. Each part of the world has its own special mixture of weather during the year. This mixture is called the climate of that region.

The seasons

In most places the weather changes throughout the year. We call these changes the seasons. In some parts of the world, there are only one or two seasons. But in other places there are four seasons – spring, summer, autumn and winter.

▷ This forest in northern America has a coastal climate – warm summers, mild winters and rain all year. In autumn, the leaves change colour and fall from the trees.

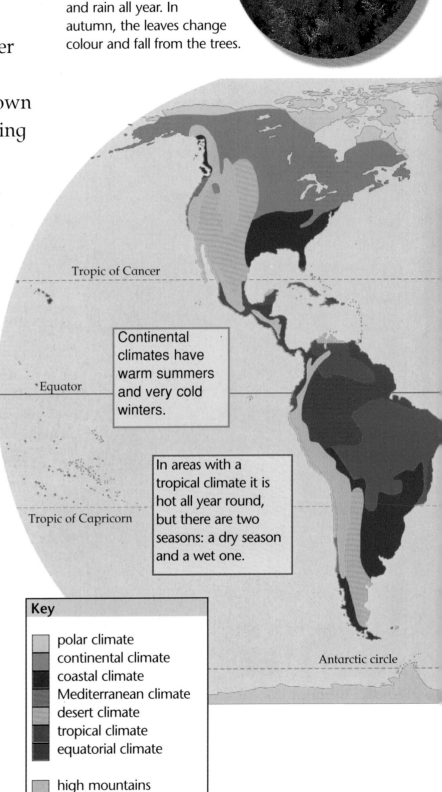

Tropic of Cancer

Continental climates have warm summers and very cold winters.

Equator

In areas with a tropical climate it is hot all year round, but there are two seasons: a dry season and a wet one.

Tropic of Capricorn

Antarctic circle

△ Hardly any rain falls on this African desert, and few plants grow. Desert climates are always very dry.

Key

- polar climate
- continental climate
- coastal climate
- Mediterranean climate
- desert climate
- tropical climate
- equatorial climate

- high mountains

▷ The Mediterranean area is hot and dry in the summer. Winters are rainy, but it is still warm.

▽ In the Asian rainforest, heavy rain and heat make the plants grow very quickly. Climates on the Equator have only one season – hot and wet.

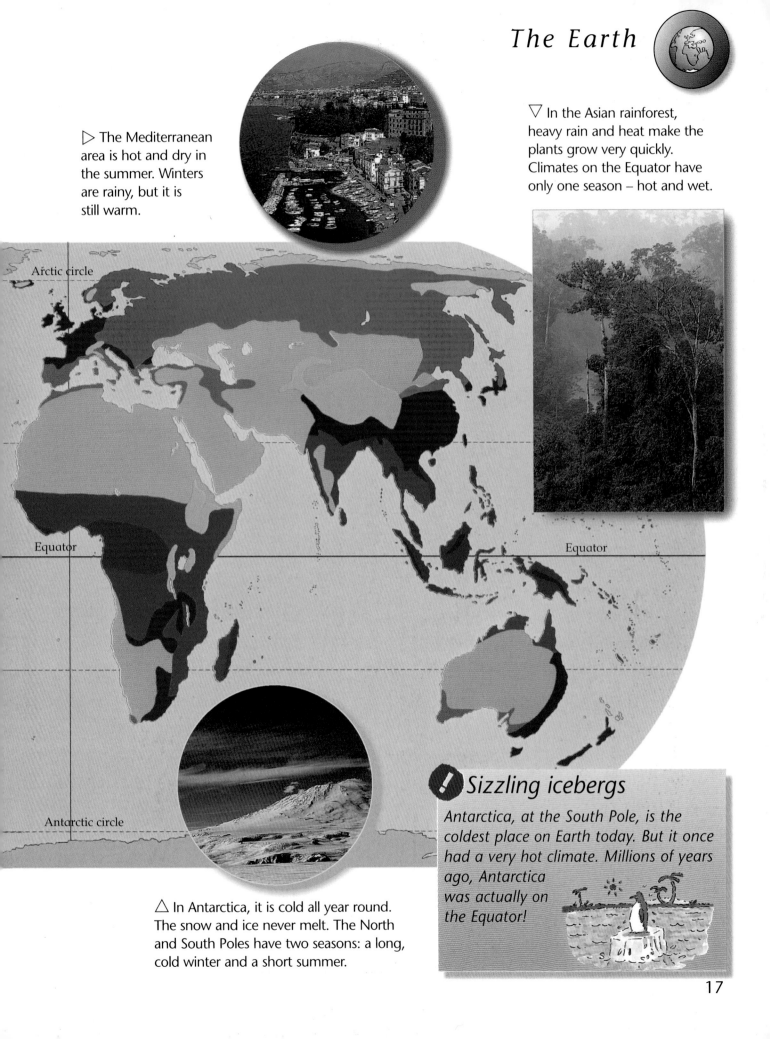

Arctic circle

Equator

Equator

Antarctic circle

△ In Antarctica, it is cold all year round. The snow and ice never melt. The North and South Poles have two seasons: a long, cold winter and a short summer.

⚠ *Sizzling icebergs*

Antarctica, at the South Pole, is the coldest place on Earth today. But it once had a very hot climate. Millions of years ago, Antarctica was actually on the Equator!

Rocks, metals and minerals

Rocks are all around you! Look for them on paths and roads, on the beach, in fields and streams, and in walls and houses. There are many different kinds of rock. They can be hard or crumbly, rough or smooth, shiny or dull. Rocks are a mixture of metals and other solid materials called minerals. Many of these metals and minerals are very useful to us.

Changing rocks

Rocks are millions of years old. Yet they are changing all the time, as the surface of the Earth changes. As some rocks are worn away by the weather, other new rocks are being made. These changes take millions of years.

△ Some rocks start as a red-hot liquid, deep inside the Earth. The liquid bursts out onto the surface through a volcano. When it cools, the liquid hardens to form rock.

△ Other rocks are formed from mud, sand or tiny pieces of broken shells. These settle in layers at the bottom of rivers, lakes or seas. As the layers slowly get thicker, the sand or mud gets squashed into rock.

△ Rocks can also be changed without being broken up first. If rocks become very hot or are squeezed and heated at the same time, they may change into a different kind of rock. These kind of changes often happen when mountains are being formed.

Rocks in your home

An amazing number of things in your home came originally from rocks. Metals are made from special types of rock called "ore". Your bike is probably made of steel, which comes from iron ore. All your cups, bowls and plates, and the wash basin in your bathroom, are made of ceramics. Ceramics come from clay, which is another kind of rock.

▷ Glass is made from special sand and a type of rock called limestone.

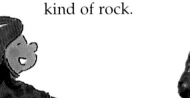

iron ore

glass-making sand

limestone

Buried treasure

Some metals and minerals are easy to find in the ground. Others are much harder. Gold and silver are rare metals. Diamonds and rubies are rare minerals. They are called precious metals and stones, and are very valuable.

△ This beautiful sword has precious metals and jewels (precious stones) in the handle.

! Animal and plant fuel

The oil and petrol that we use in our cars are made from animals! Oil is formed from the squashed bodies of animals and plants buried millions of years ago. The oil soaks into the rocks around it, like water into a sponge.

Earth in danger

The Earth is under attack – not from space aliens, but from people like us! Many of the things we do are damaging the world. People are cutting down too many trees, burning too much fuel and spreading too many dangerous chemicals. These activities are harming the Earth's animals and plants. They also harm the air we breathe and the water we drink.

heat from the Sun

escaping heat

layer of dirty air

trapped heat

harmful gases

Warming up

The air around the Earth is getting dirtier. This is because we are burning too much fuel. We fill the air with harmful gases and dirt, which makes a change in the air. The layer of dirty air around the Earth begins to trap more of the Sun's heat than before, and the Earth becomes a warmer place.

Acid rain

Cars, lorries and factory chimneys give out gases that are full of harmful chemicals. These gases rise into the air. Here they mix with rain droplets, and turn them into acid rain. When this acid rain falls to the ground, it harms plants, especially trees. It also damages buildings.

▷ This pine tree has lost all its needles because of acid rain.

The Universe

The Universe is everything out in space.
Nobody knows how big the Universe is.
To us, the Earth seems huge. Yet the Earth
is only a small planet that travels around
the Sun. The Sun itself is a star. If you look
at the sky on a clear night, you can see
thousands and thousands of other stars.
In the vast space of the Universe, the Earth
and the Sun are only tiny specks!

△ The Earth is one of nine
planets that move round
the Sun. And the Sun is just
one of the millions of stars
in the enormous Universe.

The Sun and the Moon

The Earth is a planet that travels round the Sun. We say that the Earth orbits the Sun. It takes one year (about 365 days) to go all the way round. At the same time the Moon orbits the Earth. It takes about 28 days for the Moon to go right round the Earth. The Moon is our nearest neighbour in space.

A ball of gases

The Sun is a giant ball of very hot, glowing gases. They are squeezed together so tightly that the centre of the Sun is unbelievably hot. The heat flows up to the surface and then out into space. Only a tiny part of the Sun's heat and light reach us on Earth. Even these are so powerful that you should never look directly at the Sun.

◁ Dark patches sometimes appear on the surface of the Sun. These patches are sunspots. They are areas where the surface is cooler and less bright than the rest of the Sun. A large sunspot can be bigger than the whole of the planet Earth!

No life

There is no air or water on the Moon. In fact there is no life there at all. The Moon is just a ball of rock covered with dust. On its surface there are mountains and big holes called craters.

Moon

Earth

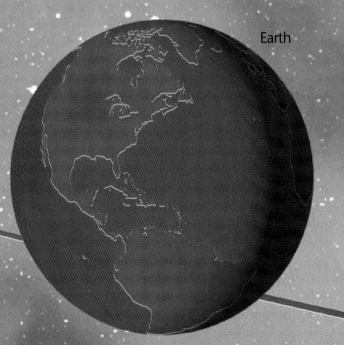

Phases of the Moon

Why does the Moon shine? It has no light of its own. All the Moon's light comes from the Sun. It is then reflected down to us on Earth. The Sun's rays always light up half of the Moon's surface. At the same time the other half is in darkness. But as the Moon travels round the Earth, we see different amounts of its bright side. It seems as if the Moon is slowly changing shape all the time. These different shapes are called the phases of the Moon.

▽ The Moon takes 28 days to go through all these phases.

| full Moon | three-quarter Moon | half Moon | crescent Moon | Moon completely hidden |

The planets

The Earth and eight other planets are all whizzing round the Sun. We call the Sun and its family of planets the Solar System. (The word solar means "of the Sun".) All nine planets in the Solar System are kept in their place by the pull of gravity. The Sun's gravity tugs on them and stops them flying off into outer space.

Nearest to furthest

All the planets in the Solar System orbit the Sun at different distances. Mercury is the nearest – and one of the hottest! Venus is next closest, and it is hot there, too. Next nearest the Sun is the Earth. Beyond the Earth are Mars, Jupiter, Saturn, Uranus, Neptune and, furthest away of all, Pluto.

△ This picture shows all the planets in the Solar System orbiting round the Sun.

Big and small

The planets in the Solar System are all different sizes. The Sun is bigger than any of them – it is over 100 times wider than the Earth. The planets are shown below in their order from the Sun.

▽ Jupiter is the biggest planet. It is mainly made of gas, but there are liquids and rock deep inside it.

▽ Mercury is one of the smallest planets. It is bare and rocky.

▽ Venus is the brightest planet in the night sky. It is covered in poisonous gases.

▽ Earth looks blue from space because so much of the surface is water.

▽ Mars is an orangey-red colour. This is because of the dust storms that blow across it.

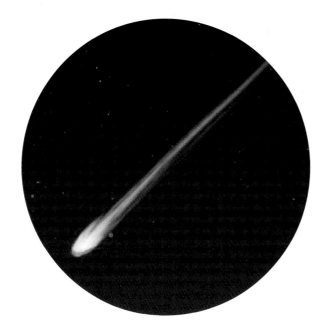

Shooting stars

Have you ever seen a sudden streak of light in the sky? It was probably a shooting star. Shooting stars are not stars at all. Lots of small pieces of rock are flying around the Solar System. Some of them rush straight towards the Earth. When they reach the atmosphere, the rocks become very hot and burn up. This burning is what you see in the sky.

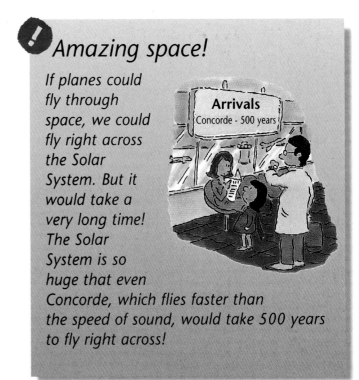

Amazing space!

If planes could fly through space, we could fly right across the Solar System. But it would take a very long time! The Solar System is so huge that even Concorde, which flies faster than the speed of sound, would take 500 years to fly right across!

Arrivals
Concorde - 500 years

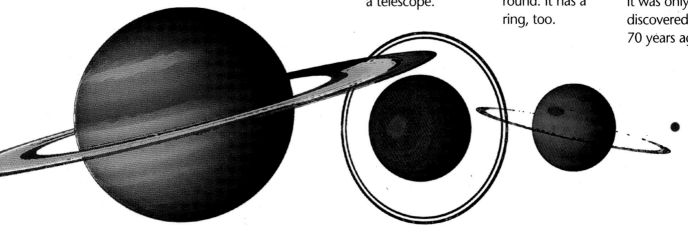

▽ Saturn has rings around it. These are made of lots of separate pieces of ice.

▽ Uranus also has rings. It was the first planet to be discovered by someone using a telescope.

▽ Neptune is so far from the Sun that it takes 165 years to go right round. It has a ring, too.

▽ Pluto is on the edge of the Solar System. It was only discovered about 70 years ago.

The stars

Have you ever tried counting the stars? It is a very difficult thing to do. There are thousands of them! Even if you could count all the stars you can see, there are millions more that you cannot see without a telescope. Every one of these stars is a glowing ball of gas, just like our Sun.

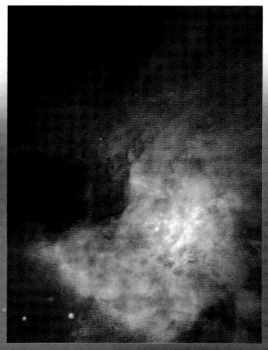

△ This cloud of gas out in space is called the Orion Nebula. One day in the future, it may become a star.

How a star is made

Where do stars come from? Out in space, there are clouds of dust and gas between the stars. As these clouds move along, they pull more dust and gas towards them. The gas is crushed tightly into a ball, and becomes very, very hot. The star is a bit like a giant power station, giving out lots of heat and light.

The Milky Way

Stars are not scattered evenly through space. They come together in enormous star groups, called galaxies. Our Sun is part of a galaxy called the Milky Way. You can easily see the Milky Way on a clear night. It stretches in a misty band right across the sky.

Shapes in the sky

If you look carefully, you can see that some bright stars make shapes in the sky. The shapes can look like animals, or like people. They have names too. There is a Great Bear and a Little Bear, a Dragon, a Scorpion and a Dog.

▽ If you live in the northern half of the world, one of the easiest star shapes to see is Orion the Hunter. You can find it by spotting three bright stars in a row – these are Orion's belt. (You can only see Orion in the winter.)

▷ If you live in the southern half of the world, you will always be able to see the Southern Cross in the night sky. Its four bright stars make the shape of a cross.

Why do stars twinkle?

When you look at a star in the sky, it seems to twinkle. In fact, the star is giving out steady beams of light. This light has to travel a very long way through space to reach us. Then it has to pass through the Earth's atmosphere, the layer of moving air that surounds our planet. The air bends and breaks up the star's beams of light - and that makes the light twinkle.

Exploring space

The Universe is a very mysterious place. We have started to explore just our own tiny corner of it. Spacecraft with people on board have landed on the Moon. Other people have spent many weeks inside space stations going round the Earth. Spacecraft with nobody on board have travelled much farther – right to the edge of the Solar System.

fuel tank

rocket booster

△ Most spacecraft are used only once. But the Space Shuttle can be used again and again. When it takes off, the Shuttle has a huge fuel tank and two rocket boosters attached to it. When the fuel runs out, these break away and fall back to Earth.

△ We can look at space through telescopes. But the dust and winds in the Earth's atmosphere get in the way. In 1990, scientists sent a telescope up into space to get a clearer look. It is called the Hubble Space Telescope. It sends us amazing pictures of faraway stars and galaxies.

Walking in space

Astronauts sometimes have to work outside their spacecraft. They wear a special suit with its own supply of oxygen so they can breathe. The backpack is really a tiny jet engine. The astronauts use it to move around outside the spacecraft.

backpack

camera

Glossary

Antarctic the area around the South Pole.

Arctic the area around the North Pole.

astronaut a person who flies in a spacecraft.

atmosphere the layer of air that surrounds the Earth.

axis a straight line around which something turns.

ceramic a material like pottery, which is made from clay that has been baked until it is hard.

climate the kind of weather that a particular area usually has.

desert an area where hardly any rain falls. Few animals and plants can live there, because it is so dry.

Equator an imaginary line right around the middle of the Earth. The hottest places in the world are near the Equator.

fossil the remains of a plant or animal from long ago. Many fossils are found inside rocks.

fuel something that is used up to produce energy, for example by burning it.

galaxy a group of millions of stars. Our Sun is in a galaxy called the Milky Way.

gravity the force that pulls objects towards the Earth.

hurricane a violent storm with heavy rain and very strong winds.

lava rock that is so hot, it is liquid. Volcanoes often spout lava when they erupt.

mineral a type of substance found in the ground, such as oil or coal.

ore a rock which is rich in one type of metal.

oxygen a gas in the air, which we need to breathe to stay alive.

planet a huge ball of rock or gas or ice that goes round and round the Sun. The Earth is a planet, and so are Mercury and Saturn.

Poles the North Pole and the South Pole. The Poles are at opposite ends of the Earth's axis. Both places are very cold, but the South Pole is coldest.

rocket a flying machine that is pushed along by a jet of hot gases. Rockets can fly in space because their engines do not need air to work.

satellite an object or a spacecraft that circles around a planet.

seasons the way that the weather changes during the year. Many places have four seasons: spring, summer, autumn and winter.

stars the tiny points of light we see in the sky at night. They are actually enormous balls of very hot gas, but they seem small because they are so far away.

tropics an area of the world close to the Equator. The weather is usually hot in the tropics.

Universe everything we know about, from the Earth, the planets and the Sun to the farthest stars and galaxies in space.

Index

Acknowledgements

Abbreviations: t = top; b = bottom; c = centre; l = left; r = right; (back) = background; (fore) = foreground.

Illustrations
Cover Julian Baum; 5 Julian Baum; 6–7 Oxford University Press; 8 Julian Baum; 8tr Scot Ritchie; 9b Julian Baum; 10bl Michael Eaton; 11tr Scot Ritchie; 12–13 Steve Lings; 13br Scot Ritchie; 14–15 Steve Lings; 14tr Scot Ritchie; 15bl Peter Joyce; 16–17 Oxford University Press; 17br Scot Ritchie; 18cl, c, cr Chris Brown; 19tl, tr Scot Ritchie; 19b Chris Brown; 20c John Haslam; 20r Peter Visscher; 21 Julian Baum; 22–23 Julian Baum; 24 Julian Baum; 25tl, b Julian Baum; 25tr Scot Ritchie; 26–27 (fore) Ellen Beier; 26–27 (back) Julian Baum; 28 Oxford Illustrators.

Photographs
The publishers would like to thank the following for permission to reproduce photographs:

9tr Robert Harding; 10–11 Science Photo Library; 11l Robert Harding; 13tr Image Bank; 15tr Science Photo Library; 16t Image Bank; 16b Natural History Photo Archive (NHPA); 17t Robert Harding; 17c Natural History Photo Archive (NHPA); 17bl B. & C. Alexander; 18bl, bc, br Geoscience Features (Dr Booth); 19 tc Geoscience Features (Dr Booth); 27t Julian Baum/NASA ; 28tr Science Photo Library.